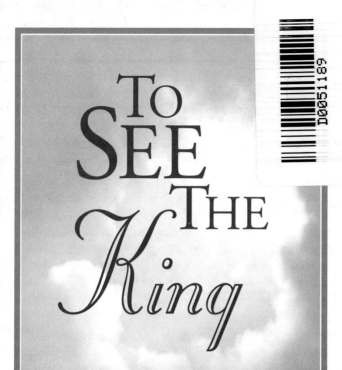

To SEE THE King

DOUG BATCHELOR

Mountain Ministry
5431 Auburn Blvd. Suite A-1
Sacramento, CA 95841

The author assumes full responsibility for the accuracy of all the
facts and quotations as cited in this book.

Condensed from *Seven Steps to Salvation—Practical ideas for
making Christ a permanent part of your life,* 1992.

This book was
Re-edited by Bonnie Ensminger
Designed and Typeset by Palimor Studios
Typeset: 11/13 Adobe Garamond

Printed in the U.S.A.

05 04 03 02 01   5 4 3 2 1

Library of Congress Cataloging-in-Publication Data:
Batchelor, Doug, 1957 —
            To See the King—Seven Steps to Salvation
            1. Christian Life. 2. Salvation.

ISBN 0-9668105-1-1

TO SEE THE KING
Seven Steps to Salvation

CONTENTS

Dedicated to
my brother, Falcon

$\mathcal{I}$NTRODUCTION

There's no better tool for teaching a point than a good story! This book is based on the conversion, cleansing and call of Isaiah found in the first eight verses of Isaiah 6. It is not intended to be an exhaustive study but rather a springboard I will use to share the process of salvation through personal experiences, stories and observations. The Bible, too, is a storybook, and every story or parable in the Bible teaches us something about God's plan to save people from misery and death.

Isaiah's ministry as a royal prophet was long and fruitful, spanning over sixty years and touching the lifetime of five kings. Isaiah married a prophetess, and they had two sons. Jewish tradition tells us he died a martyr's death. Hezekiah's wicked son, King Manasseh, had Isaiah placed in a hollow log and sawn in half (Hebrews 11:37).

Isaiah's name means, "Yahweh saves," or "God saves." Of all the Old Testament prophets, Isaiah most beautifully and clearly describes the ministry and mission of the coming Messiah and Savior.

Our passage in this book is the only recorded vision in Isaiah's writings. In just eight verses it gives us an inspiring and comprehensive picture of the process of his conversion. A baby needs to roll over before he can crawl, crawl before he can walk and walk before he can run. Likewise there is a process to salvation—a sequence, an order of events–that is elementary.

I have divided the story of Isaiah 6:1-8 into seven steps with illustrations. We need to understand this simple sequence in our walk with the Lord for both ourselves and for sharing salvation with others. Here it is, from the New King James version:

Isaiah 6:1-8

*In the year that King Uzziah died, (1) **I saw the Lord** sitting on a throne, high and lifted up, and the train of His robe filled the temple.*

Above it stood seraphim; each one had six wings; with two he covered his face, with two he covered his feet, and with two he flew.

And one cried to another and said: "Holy, holy, holy is the Lord of hosts; the whole earth is full of His glory!"

And the posts of the door were shaken by the voice of him who cried out, and the house was filled with smoke.

*So I said: (2) **'Woe is me, for I am undone!** (3) **Because I am a man of unclean lips,** and (4) **I dwell in the midst of a people of unclean lips;** for my eyes have seen the King, the Lord of hosts.'*

Then one of the seraphim flew to me, having in his hand a live coal which he had taken with the tongs from the altar.

*And he touched my mouth with it, and said: "Behold, this has touched your lips; (5) **your iniquity is taken away, and your sin is purged."***

*(6) **Also I heard the voice of the Lord saying:*** *"Whom shall I send, and who will go for us?"*

*Then I said, (7) **"Here am I. Send me.**"*

It is my sincere prayer that this short work will assist you in knowing the steps of salvation and in taking them, so you, too, may know the Lord and walk with Him!

D.E.B.

STEP *1*

TO *See* GOD

*"In the year that King Uzziah
died, I saw the Lord."*
Isaiah 6:1

A Vision of God

W hen I was growing up in New York City,
it was a "cool" thing to make fun of the police. We
called them "pigs." We took great pride in sharing
stories of how we had insulted a cop without getting
caught. One time while I was driving a stolen car, I
pulled up to an officer and asked him for directions
just so that a friend and I could later laugh at him.
Cops were the "enemy."

But my whole attitude about the police
changed one night, when, flipping through the TV
channels, I happened to see a very graphic news story.
A building was on fire. The camera was capturing all
the drama of the firefighters rushing in and out,
spraying water on the building. People were trying to
climb off the roof on to a ladder. Then one of the

11

cameras focused on the main entrance to the building, which by this point was engulfed in flames with smoke billowing out the windows and doors.

Suddenly an officer came running out the door with a blanket in his arms. Smoke was coming off his singed clothes. The firemen hosed him off as he rushed through the crowd to an open spot and laid the bundle he was carrying on the grass and unwrapped it. Inside was a baby—unconscious. Completely ignoring his own burns, the officer proceeded to administer artificial respiration seeking to revive the unconscious infant. My whole concept of policemen as the enemy changed when I saw that he was willing to risk his life to save the people he served. Suddenly, I realized that maybe I was the bad guy and the police were the good guys.

That's the way it is with God. For many years I thought God was against me—a great big policeman up in the sky, watching and waiting to see me doing something wrong so He could thump me with His billy club! He was there to restrict my happiness. But then I saw a new picture of Jesus dying to save me. John 10:10 says, "I have come that you may have life and have it more abundantly" (paraphrased), and I realized that Jesus only wants us to give up the things that hurt us!

Ninety per cent of all the information that comes into our brains comes through our eyes. Most of us consider that sight is the most important of our five senses. Even in the Bible Jesus compares our eyes to spiritual understanding and discernment, saying that if the blind lead the blind, they will both fall into the ditch (Matthew 15:14). One of Jesus' frequent miracles was to open the eyes of the blind.

I think the reason so many people have trouble being Christians and staying Christians is that they don't know where to begin. Wherever I go I ask people what they think is the first step in salvation. Even people who have been church members for fifty years will usually say the steps are: repent, believe, accept, and confess that you are a sinner. But I don't believe that any of these is step number one!

The first step in the process of salvation always begins with Seeing the Lord in His holiness and in the year our Savior died.

John 1:29 tells us that one day when John the Baptist saw Jesus walking by the Jordan River, he pointed to Him and said, "Behold! The Lamb of God who takes away the sin of the world!" Later, two of John's disciples said to Jesus, "Rabbi, . . . where are You staying?" He said to them, "Come and see" (John 1:38, 39). In that same chapter of John, when Philip came to Nathaniel, he said, "We have found the Messiah, Jesus of Nazareth" (Paraphrased).

Nathaniel didn't argue back. Philip said, "Come and see." (verse 46). In fact just in the first chapter of John there are over 26 references to light and sight! We are finding again and again that we need to see the Lord! Even when we go to the end of the Gospels and look at the thief who died on the cross next to Jesus, we find all the steps in salvation (Luke 23:34). He saw Jesus hanging on the cross. He probably heard Jesus say, "Father, forgive them, for they do not know what they do." As the thief

13

watched all these acts and deeds of kindness with no hostility or aggression, seeing God's goodness helped the thief become aware of his own badness. You see, the Bible tells us it's the goodness of God that leads us to repentance. "I have heard of You by the hearing of the ear, but now my eye sees You," Job said. "Therefore I abhor myself, and repent in dust and ashes" (Job 42:5,6). Even the apostle Paul was converted as a result of seeing Jesus on the road to Damascus (Acts 9:1-9).

Now you may be thinking, "didn't Jesus plainly say, 'Blessed are those who have not seen and yet have believed.'" (John 20:29). Yes, He did, but He was speaking of people who keep demanding some physical sign or 3-D vision. But when I speak of seeing God in this book, I'm not suggesting that you fast and pray until you have some angelic visitation or a personal revelation of the Almighty in technicolor. I'm talking about the eye of faith.

When Jesus arose from the dead, the Bible says the disciples were overjoyed when they saw the Lord (John 20:20). As Christians, our greatest joy will come from seeing that the Lord is alive and with us always! The Bible tells us in the story of Zacchaeus that he wanted so much to see Jesus–who He was–that he climbed a tree (Luke 19:1-10). When he saw Jesus' goodness, and when he saw that Jesus accepted him, he then saw his own sins. He repented, he confessed, and he was willing to pay back. And Jesus said that salvation had come to him. All this happened very quickly <u>after he saw the Lord</u>. Yet I believe that even though Zacchaeus first saw the Lord after He climbed a tree, his clearest vision of the Lord came when Jesus climbed the tree and died for him! Incidentally the name Zacchaeus means "Pure" and didn't Jesus say, "Blessed are the pure in heart, for they shall see God" (Matthew 5:8)?

When we see God on the cross, when we see God in that year that our king died, then we are more willing to love Him and to serve Him. This is the first step–TO SEE GOD!

You are What You See

I really worry about young people today. Throughout my childhood I had what I would consider normal American heroes. I always pictured myself being like Daniel Boone or Davy Crockett. (I will confess, though, there was a period in my life when I hoped I could be like Superman!)

A few years ago one of my boys was telling me about Teenage Mutant Ninja Turtles. These childhood heroes live in the sewers of New York City and eat pizza! I think our country is in big trouble if our kids want to grow up to be mutant Ninja turtles that live in the sewer! The folk proverb, "You are what you eat," is also true of your mental intake.

There's a biblical principle in that we become like what we worship or behold. "But we all, with unveiled face, beholding as in a mirror the glory of the Lord, are being transformed into the same image…"

(2 Corinthians 3:18). I think that's the main reason for all of the violent, unstable behavior in our young people. They spend so much time watching violence, deception and sex on television that it can't help but have some definite effect on their lives.

A few months ago, I was preaching in a small church in northern California. After the service, my wife and I were invited over to a member's home for dinner. Another guest at this meal was very interesting. His name was Joe and he related a tragic testimony.

Some years ago when Elvis Presley was first beginning his career, Joe went to a concert, and he was overwhelmed with the way all the women fell down, took off their clothes, and swooned as Elvis gyrated his pelvis and sang. Something snapped in his mind, and he thought, I'd like to be just like Elvis Presley.

When I was growing up, my mother used to write songs for Elvis Presley, so I saw him a couple of times in person. I was not very impressed!

Not long after seeing Elvis, Joe went home and purchased all of his records. He wallpapered his room with Elvis Presley posters. He dyed his hair black and bought a guitar. He stood in front of a mirror hour after hour and tried to look like Elvis and sing like Elvis. He listened to the records again and again, never growing tired of hearing his idol croon.

Any time Elvis had a concert within three or four hundred miles, Joe was there! He went to all of the Elvis Presley movies, filled his house with Elvis paraphernalia and what's even more pathetic, he did this for twenty years. Think of it–twenty years idolizing, imitating and worshipping Elvis Presley!

By the time Elvis died, Joe had become so good at imitating him that he started working in nightclubs around the country. He began making thousands of dollars a week for his imitation of Elvis. People who saw him said it was eerie, because Joe seemed just like Elvis. He sang just like Elvis, he walked like Elvis, and he played the guitar like Elvis.

When I met Joe, he was probably nearing fifty years of age. Elvis had already been dead for over ten years, yet Joe was still making up to $10,000 a concert in the Orient imitating Elvis Presley.

Joe had come to church in this small Northern California town for a little while hoping to break away from his old life. He had Christian roots as a child. He told me, "I don't even have my own identity. I have been living like someone else for so long that I don't know who I am." So after a short time trying to go to church, Joe felt he had nothing else to fall back on and returned to imitating Elvis Presley!

I couldn't help but wonder what kind of church we would have if we all idolized Jesus Christ the way Joe idolized Elvis Presley! He's the only individual in the Bible we are encouraged to worship and idolize. If we spend all our time looking at Teenage Mutant Ninja Turtles or watching soap operas like, "As the Stomach Turns," (or whatever it's called) then we're going to be a mental mess. But if we spend our time looking at Jesus every day, we cannot help but become like Him!

We need to see God.

Evidence of God

There are many ways to see God. His Word, of course, is the most reliable. God also reveals Himself to us through other people and through the things He has made. Our passage in Isaiah tells us these angelic creatures in the presence of God called out, "The whole earth is full of His glory" (Isaiah 6:3)!

But many people cannot see the Lord through the things He has made because their vision has been obscured by the cataracts of evolution.

One of the big struggles I had in accepting Christ, and the Bible in particular, was that I grew up believing in evolution. Virtually all the schools I attended taught that people are nothing more than a highly developed strain of monkey. That doesn't offer much purpose for life, does it! If we just evolved from a primeval puddle of mud somewhere, and if, when people die, they just turn back into fertilizer, then there's really no purpose to life. I believe this false teaching of evolution is largely responsible for the high rate of suicide among teenagers. What can we expect if we tell them life is nothing more than a biological burp? I am convinced that everyone's philosophy is affected by our environment–by the things which surround us.

Growing up in New York City, I was continually enclosed by things man made. I heard the screeching of brakes and the roar of traffic. Wherever I looked I saw concrete and glass, flashing lights, and the things that man has made. I came to the place where I put my trust in people. And since people were telling me we just evolved, I believed it.

Then, as a teenager, I spent about a year and a half living in a cave outside of Palm Springs, California. There I began to get a whole different perspective on life. I was now surrounded by the things that God made, and it had a profound influence on me.

Whenever you look through a microscope at the things we humans make, you can see flaws and mistakes. But when you look through that same microscope at the things God made, you see infinite perfection. We have two choices. Even the scientists know this. We're either here by accident–by things blowing up–or we're here because of an intelligent design and a plan.

When I went to school in New York City, I remember asking my science teacher one day, "Where did the world come from?" He told me in essence that the world came from the sun when it exploded and developed into our solar system.

"Well," I asked, "Where did the sun come from?"

He said the sun came from another galaxy. When the Milky Way galaxy was formed, there was an explosion out there from two gas masses that ran into each other and exploded.

And then I asked, "Where did the gas masses come from?"

I know it doesn't sound scientific to say that matter can create itself, but ultimately, even scientists have to acknowledge that something has always existed. We can look at all the organization and design that we see around us and believe that it all came from gas particles that always existed and started exploding, or we can believe that there is an intelligent God and Creator, and He's always existed. I think it is more logical to believe that my roots go back to a loving heavenly Father and not two gas masses and particles floating out there in the universe that accidentally collided one day and blew up.

When you look at all the evidence in nature, even intelligent people need to agree that there is a Master Planner.

A friend of mine, Dr. Lolita Simpson, walked up to me one day to show me a flower. She said, "Doug, I want to show you something. See this flower?" I thought, "Isn't this sweet, this dear old saint is going to show me a flower."

But she showed it to me through the eyes of a scientist. She said, "Now here you see five petals, and they're surrounded by five leaves, and inside are five little stems, and it's all perfectly symmetrical. There's organization, there's design and fragrance too. This could never happen by accident."

Design, organization, and plan do not come out of chaos. That would be like suggesting that you could throw a bomb into a junkyard and get a Boeing 747 when the dust settled; or that you could throw another bomb into a print shop and get an *Encyclopedia Britannica!* The most simple form of single cell life, when carefully studied, revels more complexity than New York City at rush hour!

Even if we could come to the place where we

believe that everything evolved, and if micro-organisms did just start splitting, dividing and growing into larger forms of life, then, I wondered, where did the need for male and female come from? When people get ready to start a family, why don't they just start splitting and dividing? Isn't that how they say it all happened? Why would there ever be the need for two completely different genders, male and female, that could not reproduce without an act of love and cooperation?

And what about the birds? I'm a pilot, and I know a little about aerodynamic design. Back when I believed in evolution, I was somehow able to picture these sea creatures slowly developing arms and legs and crawling farther and farther out of the water for longer periods of time. But I always had a problem picturing lizards running off cliffs, trying to develop aerodynamic design with feathers and hollow bones before they hit the ground. And then, if they did hit the ground and survive, how could they pass it on to their offsprings?

After they are hatched, many birds develop feathers and jump out of the nest. Then bingo, they know how to fly and play on the air currents with no lessons at all. The tiny little caterpillar spins a cocoon around itself, and within a week or so it emerges, pumps blood into its new wings, fans them a few times, and takes off to play on the air. The suggestions that all these things happened by accident seems all the more ludicrous and outrageous.

Two friends were walking in a parking lot together. One believed in creation and God, and the other believed in evolution and the scientist. The evolutionist said to his creationist friend, "Oh, I see you got a new car! Where did you get it?"

His Christian friend shrewdly responded, "Well, I went out into my garage one day and there was this puddle of oil. I left it alone. Over a period of weeks, as I watched, gradually a skateboard oozed up out of the pavement, then it slowly evolved into a VW bug. I drove it for a while and pretty soon it turned into a Pinto, and ultimately it developed into this Honda Accord!"

Of course the evolutionist responded, "Cut it out. Where did you get your car?"

His creationist friend said, "Now wait a second. You don't believe that my car oozed up out of the pavement, because you know that when you see a car with organization, design, planning, and working systems, somewhere there is a car maker. Just because all the different cars and all the different road-traveling vehicles have tires, headlights and windshield wipers doesn't mean that one evolved from the other."

Ford did not evolve from Chevy and Chevy didn't evolve from Chrysler. They all share things in common because they operate in a common environment. In the same way, there may be similarities between men and monkeys and other creatures, but that doesn't mean we all evolved from each other. It means we all share the same environment. And so God gave us certain things in common.

When you see a car, you know right away that

out there somewhere is a car maker. The human being is a far more complex machine than any automobile, so likewise, we know that somewhere there is a "people maker."

In many of His parables, Jesus turns our attention to the things God made (Matthew 6:26). Even in this world tainted by sin, we can see abundant evidence of God's power, wisdom, and love through the things He created (Romans 1:20).

The whole earth is full of His glory, and we can see God through the things he has made, but we need to take the time to look.

STEP 2

TO SEE YOURSELF

"Woe is me, for I am undone!"
Isaiah 6:5

The Black Rainbow

I remember when I was about four years old, my father had a chrome machine in his hall he used for shining his shoes. It had a motor with a red furry wheel on one side and a black furry wheel on the other side. (He still has it!) There was a button on top, and every morning before he went to work, he stepped on the bottom, and the brushes would begin to spin. He would stick his shoes underneath and buff them, step on the button again to stop the machine, and then go off to work.

I was extremely fascinated with Dad's shoeshine machine. Sometimes I would sit in the hall captivated by just pushing the buttons on and off. I liked to put my hand on the furry brushes and feel them whirl around.

One Sunday morning I woke up before everyone else. I wandered around the house looking for something to do, not daring to wake up my father on his day off! I sat in the hall and begin playing with the shoeshine machine. After turning it on and off for a while, I got bored with that game. So I thought, "Why don't I shine Dad's shoes?" I quietly opened my father's bedroom door, tiptoed in, picked up his black shoes, tiptoed out and shut the door.

I knew to get them really shiny I would have to use some shoe polish. I remembered seeing some under the bathroom sink.

So I checked, and sure enough, there was a bottle of black, liquid Griffin shoe polish. I went back out in the hall to the shoeshine machine. I wasn't altogether sure what the sequence was, but I felt pretty certain that the black shoe polish went on the black brush. I poured a generous amount of black liquid shoe polish on the black brush. I wanted Dad's shoes very shiny. Then I turned on the machine.

At first it shook like a washing machine out of balance on the spin cycle, spitting shoe polish everywhere. Then it began to turn at hurricane velocity, spraying a nice, even black rainbow of shoe polish right up the wall, across the ceiling, and back down the other side of the wall.

Seeing what had happened, I decided it must be time for me to go back to sleep! I quickly turned the machine off, toddled back into the bedroom, and jumped into bed. My brother and a stepbrother were also living in the house, so I comforted myself with the knowledge that no one would know which one of us did it because no one saw me!

After a few endless and agonizing minutes I heard my father moving around in the bedroom, and I listened anxiously as the bedroom door opened. I had already decided I would pretend to be asleep. I could hear him walk around in the hall for a minute, and then I heard a gasp...a pause...and then he called out my name. "Dougie, Dougie, get in here!"

I wondered why he was calling my name. "Nobody saw me," I thought. "I'll just act like I'm asleep."

Petty soon my bedroom door swung open, and Dad walked in. "Dougie, get up," he said.

As well as a four year old could, I tried to fake that I had been asleep, but somehow I don't think he was convinced.

I sheepishly marched off into the hall. The black rainbow loomed above me as menacing as ever. I failed to mention that not only did it go up the wall, but it went right through the middle of an expensive picture of a Spanish conquistador!

"Do you know anything about this?" my Dad said with glaring eyes. It would have been a good time to 'fess up, but that little demonic voice inside my head said, "Nobody saw you. He won't know." So I said, "No."

Dad said, "I'll ask you again, do you know anything about this?"

I wanted to tell the truth, but I thought I would try to bluff one more time. I was sealing my doom. Once you start on the road to deception, it's hard to turn back. "No," I said, trying to sound more convincing.

"All right," he said, "I'm going to spank you until you tell the truth." In a flash, he pulled down my pants, threw me over his knee, and commenced spanking me. As I felt his hand stinging against my posterior, I shouted, "I didn't do it! I didn't do it! I didn't do it! I did it! I did it! I did it!" One can only take so much torture before he breaks.

My father set me down and said, "Doug, I'm not punishing you for making a mistake. I spanked you because you lied to me." Then he told me to march into the bathroom and wash my face. I limped into the bathroom whimpering and climbed up on a stool (I was still too short to reach the sink without assistance), and looked into the mirror. To my amazement, I had little black spots of shoe polish all over my face! I thought nobody knew. But after my encounter with my father, I got a true picture of myself and I saw how I really looked through his eyes! Like Isaiah, I found out that I was undone!

Now let me ask you, when I looked into the mirror and saw the spots on my face, was the mirror the problem? No, I was!

In the same way, when we see Jesus on the cross for our sins, we realize we are sinners. The Bible says sin is the transgression of the law (1 John 3:4). God's law or the ten commandments are the mirror (James 1:23-25). The law is not there to take away our sins any more than the mirror washes away the dirt. The law shows us the sin; then we go to Jesus for cleansing.

Some people look at the law of God and see that there's sin in their life, and they think the answer is to throw away the ten commandments. But the ten commandments don't need changing, we do. God's law helps us see the "spots on our face." This is the second step in salvation.

Isaiah realized he was undone after he saw his heavenly Father. One sure way to know that you are becoming a Christian is that sometimes you'll sense a feeling of conviction. That's a good signal that you're on track with God. Remember, when a doctor delivers a baby, he knows it's OK when he hears it cry. Likewise, the best evidence that you have experienced a spiritual birth or rebirth, is when you cry, "Woe is me; I am a sinner."

Knowing You're Naked

When I was about 17 I lived for about a year and a half as a hermit in a mountain cave above Palm Springs. I never wore any clothes. At first, I noticed something was missing. But after going naked for several weeks, I didn't even think about it anymore. You can get used to almost anything if you do it long enough.

Once or twice a week I would hike down to Palm Springs to panhandle for money in front of Mayfair Market. I always carried my clothes in a little bundle in the bottom of my backpack. I would generally stop at a big rock on the outskirts of town and put on my clothes before venturing into the city limits. As you might have guessed, I didn't have to do laundry very often!

I remember distinctly waking up one morning, enthusiastic about going to town. I had some money in hand and I had an exciting list of things I wanted to get. When I reached the top of the ridge, I felt exhilarated! The sun was just rising and everything was glowing with a beautiful brazen color–all the hills, the cactus, and even my skin seemed to look golden.

I be-bopped down the mountain, playing my flute as I hiked toward Palm Springs. I was just so enthralled with being alive and so deep in thought that I didn't realize I had walked right past the big rock where I usually put on my clothes. I also didn't notice I was venturing into the city limits of Palm Springs with nothing on but a backpack, some hiking boots and a smile.

Suddenly, I came around a bend in the trail and saw what looked like a Mexican family–a nicely dressed father, mother and two little girls. As I recall, this was a Sunday morning, because it appeared they were dressed up and out for an early walk before church. As I came around the bend and saw them, I offered a friendly wave and a grin. But, abruptly, I noticed a shocked reaction rip through the entire family at the same time. They all froze!

The mother closed her eyes and turned her

head. The father pulled her head to his chest with his hand. Each of the two little girls grabbed one of their father's legs, turned away and closed their eyes. And then, the father closed his eyes too! I assumed there must have been some terrifying hideous monster looming behind me.

I instinctively turned around thinking, "What have they seen that made them react with such horror?" Then it finally dawned on me that I had no clothes on! Blushing from bow to stern, I slid behind the next bush on the trail and quickly put on my clothes!

What happened there? I felt just fine the moment before I saw this family. They never touched me. They said nothing to me. Yet, after that encounter, I felt awful. What made the difference? I saw myself through their eyes, and I saw that I was naked.

I think it would be healthy for Christians to get a fresh look at themselves through God's eyes. We might just discover that we are naked, too!

The Bible says this is one of the problems with God's church in the last days. Actually, the problem is not that we're naked, but that we're naked and don't know it. He says, "(You) do not know that you are wretched, miserable, poor, blind and naked" (Revelation 3:17).

We're living in a society that is very aware of psychology. Everywhere we turn people are being told, don't feel bad. Guilt is bad. Guilt is destructive. There is, of course, some truth to that. But people ought to feel guilty when they are guilty. We shouldn't feel good when we're doing something bad. The Lord wants us to feel guilt and conviction long enough to come to Him for forgiveness. He doesn't want us to remain in the state of perpetual mourning, but we must become aware of our condition before God. We must be sorry for our sins and recognize our wretched state. Then God can activate His power in our lives.

"Humble yourselves in the sight of the Lord, and He will lift you up" (James 4:10).

When Adam and Eve disobeyed God, the light that covered them went out and they became aware of their nakedness (Genesis 3:10). They tired to cover themselves with fig leaves, but soon saw the leaves would not last. After they acknowledged their guilt to God, He gave them coats of skins. Did you catch that? Skins! Something had to die to cover their naked bodies just as Jesus had to die to cover our sins.

When the prodigal son came home, his father received him, embraced him, kissed him, then covered his filth and nakedness with his own "best" robe. Jesus is waiting to clothe us with His righteousness, but we must first come home as we are.

STEP 3

TO REPENT

"Because I am a man of unclean lips."
Isaiah 6:5

Just One Little Mouse

For several years, at my home in the hills, I parked my car in a little carport, the same area where I fed my dogs. On one occasion, when starting the engine and turning on the air conditioner fan, I heard a rattling sound, and then plop, plop. A couple of little nuggets of dry dog food fell out of the vent down by my feet.

It's amazing the ridiculous things that go through our minds, but I thought to myself, "How do you like that? They must feed the same kind of dry food to their dogs in Japan (where my car was made) as I feed my dogs!"

I was busy at the time, and it never really occurred to me how dog food could have made its way into the ventilation system of my car. I didn't think it needed any further investigating. After all, two little nuggets of dog food was not that big a problem compared with other heavy issues I was dealing with from day to day. So I went on my way.

A few days later, I again hopped in the car, started it up, and heard a rattling in the fan, and plop, plop, plop, plop. Four or five dog food nuggets fell out at my feet. I realized at this point there must be a mouse or something that had moved into the ventilation system of my car and set up house. I said to myself, "I will have to take care of that someday." Well, you know how those "someday" plans are. Tomorrow never comes!

Several weeks went by and every time I started the car, more and more dog food would tumble out. Eventually it got to the place where I would be driving down the road and when I turned on the fan, I received not only dog food, but bits of mouse nest as well.

One cold day I took a long trip and unconsciously decided to turn the heater up to high. Big mistake! It wasn't just Mr. Mouse, but Mrs. Mouse and all their little mice that were living in my car. With the heater on high, five or six little naked baby mice began to crawl out of the vents. Now, I was really worried! It seems the whole family did not make it out alive.

Someone told me wild mice can have thirteen babies in a litter and I think I cooked half the family! I don't know if you have ever had the dubious privilege of smelling mummified mouse! It isn't pleasant! From that point on, the odor from the decomposing mice became so offensive that I had to drive with the ventilation off.

As summer approached, I kept putting off dealing with the problem. I would just keep the windows rolled down so I wouldn't need to turn on the air conditioning.

One hot day while driving with my friend, John Lomacang, (I had not warned him about the mouse family that had died in the remote recesses of my car's ventilation system), without consulting me, reached over, turned the fan to high and pressed the air conditioning button. Something terrible happened! Mouse nest, mouse droppings and mouse fur began to blow out with hurricane velocity in our faces, filling the car with a swirling stench and dusty debris. From that point on, whenever John and I took a trip, he insisted that we use his car.

Now think about this. I had a brand new car with cruise control, power steering, AM/FM radio and cassette, four-wheel drive–almost everything you could ask for in a new vehicle. It was shiny on the outside, but it stank on the inside because one little mouse had ruined the whole thing. One little mouse that I had not dealt with soon enough, and it messed up my whole new car.

I'm sure you get the point. It's these little sins in our lives that we let go unchecked–whether it's our temper or our words or some other habit–that work like termites on the foundation of our experience.

There's a story in the Bible in which King

David made a little mistake of looking at a woman taking a bath. Because of that lingering lustful look, that little sin turned into adultery, deception and eventually murder. He also lost four of his sons and the respect of his people for that choice. These little sins end up dragging us down. That's why if we are faithful in little things, we will be faithful in much. (Matthew 25:21)

It's interesting that the most ferocious animal in the world also happens to be the smallest—the shrew. It's smaller than a mouse, yet it can kill many animals much larger than itself. It eats the equivalent of several times its own body weight in one day. Yet, it can fit easily in a teaspoon. Little things can be deadly!

There seems to be a trend in the church today to ignore the little details of Christian faithfulness. When someone talks about "little sins," he is accused of being petty or legalistic.

Ben Franklin said:

> *"For the want of a nail, the horseshoe was lost.*
> *For the want of a shoe, the horse was lost.*
> *For the want of a horse, the rider was lost.*
> *For the want of a rider, the battle was lost.*
> *For the want of a battle, the kingdom was lost.*
> *All for the want of a nail."*

Since I am in the ministry, I have occasions when I have the responsibility to address inconsistencies in people's lives when they are professing Christ. The Bible teaches that we are our brothers' keepers, but sometimes I'm met with the words, "you're judging me." But Jesus says there is a time when we should care about the sins of our brothers.

Isaiah cared. Not only did he confess his sins, but he confessed the sins of his people. He did this, not for the purpose of making himself look better, but because he hurt for the sins of those around him. He was concerned for their welfare.

You notice in our story that Isaiah first said, "I am a man of unclean lips," and then he said, "I dwell in the midst of a people of unclean lips." That's the proper sequence. In most cases, we have 20/20 vision when it comes to spotting every little defect in the lives of others. But we are oblivious to the major problems in our own lives. That's why Jesus said, we need to be careful that we get the log out of our own eye before trying to pick a speck out of someone else's eye (Matthew 7:1-5).

In many cases, the individuals who are the most critical of those around them, have a secret sin in their own lives. Pointing to the sins of others and criticizing everybody around them is a diversionary tactic. They hope this will direct attention away from their own guilt. Isaiah was convicted that he had a problem with unclean lips. He knew he had trouble with the things he said.

Many Christians fail to pay attention to what they say because they think their words are so small. But Jesus tells us that in the judgment we will give an account for every idle word we speak. By our words we will be justified and by our word we will be condemned (Matthew 12:36, 37).

A few misplaced words can cause a whole forest fire of problems (James 3:5).   In the same way, a little word of encouragement or a smile can change the course of a person's day or even his life! (Proverbs 25:11) It's the little sins in our lives that we don't deal with and give heed to daily, that grow until they destroy our lives altogether.

The way to climb a mountain is one step at a time. If the Lord were to show us right now all the changes we need to make in our lives to be in perfect harmony with His will, it would overwhelm us. But, He leads us one day at a time, one step at a time. The way a person loses or gains weight is one bite at a time. I'm bald now and it happened one hair at a time!

Life operates on little things. Jesus told us to pray each day for our daily bread–one day at a time–because we can only handle things in little segments. The way we get to heaven is by walking with Jesus and trusting Him one moment at a time.

Sorry Enough to Stop

One day a turtle was walking through the woods when he heard a desperate voice calling, "Help, help." He soon found a frog at the bottom of a deep hole.

"What happened?" asked the turtle.

"I wasn't watching where I was hopping, and I fell into this pit," the frog croaked. "Try as I might, I just can't hop high enough to get out."

The turtle calmly asked how he could help the frog.

"If you can get me a stick and drop it in, I can climb out," the frog said.

"OK," the turtle replied, and he slowly plodded off to find a long stick. After a couple of hours the turtle returned with a stick in his mouth to find the frog sunbathing on the edge of a nearby pond. "What happened?" the turtle asked slowly. "I thought you couldn't get out of that hole."

"I couldn't," said the frog, "but a snake crawled into the hole and I had to get out!"

In the same way, we are all sorry that we have hopped into Satan's pit and often feel there's no way out until we realize what a person can do when his life depends on it. We're all sorry for our sins, but we're more sorry when we realize the penalty is death, and it already cost Jesus His life.

Don't misunderstand, I don't believe that we hop out of sin's hole by our own strength. The Bible says that without Christ we can do nothing (John 15:5). But we must have a will, a desire to be free. We should flee from temptation (1 Timothy 6:11), but many crawl away, hoping it will catch up with them! True repentance means we are not only sorry for our sins, but we're sorry enough to stop doing them. Some people think you can go to church once a week, confess your sins, and then you will have a clean slate to fill up with sin for another week. That's not true repentance!

The Bible speaks of two kinds of repentance.

Judas repented, and then he went out and hung himself (Matthew 27:4, 5). Peter repented, went out and wept bitterly, and the same night was converted (Matthew 26:75). He changed! God wants us to be sorry for our sins. Sorry enough to stop doing them. Sorry enough to change.

It's like two children I heard about who were watching their mother bake chocolate chip cookies. As she placed the warm cookies on the counter, the phone rang. Mother rushed off to answer the phone, but before leaving, she told the children not to eat the cookies.

Well, Johnny and Jane looked at and smelled those warm chocolate chip cookies. Jane noticed there was one cookie crumb. She reasoned to herself, "That's not a whole cookie. It's just a crumb." So she reached up and ate the one crumb on the plate.

Johnny, of course, felt irritated that there were no crumbs for him. So to be fair he created a crumb. He broke off a piece and ate it. He made more crumbs in the process, so now Jane had more crumbs. Back and forth they went until soon they'd eaten two or three cookies.

Then they heard Mother's footsteps approaching the kitchen, and they quietly put their hands behind their backs trying to look as innocent as possible. Even though they had chocolate residue around the edges of their mouths, Mother didn't say anything. She hoped they'd confess to what they had done. That's how it is with God. He already knows our sins. He's hoping that we will confess them willingly.

Eventually Jane was overcome with a sense of guilt. She said, "Mother, I'm sorry. I just meant to eat one crumb, but I ate some cookies." And then she added, "Johnny ate some cookies, too."

Of course Johnny quickly said, "I'm sorry, I'm sorry."

Do you see the difference? Jane was sorry she hurt and disobeyed her mother. Johnny was sorry he got caught!

Sometimes we repent because we're in trouble, and we want forgiveness. We want to go to heaven. But we're not sorry we sinned. The first chance we have, we're likely to do it again. I think it would be healthy for us to pray, "Lord, help me to truly repent."

The Bible tells us in Romans 2:4 that God is the one who gives us repentance. We can't even repent on our own. His goodness leads us to real repentance. When we see God in His goodness, it makes us truly sorry for what our sins have done to Him.

When we see Jesus hanging on the cross, he's not just hanging on any cross. He's hanging on my cross. I'm Barabbas. Those nails are my nails. That spear and those thorns all belong to me. When we see that He took what we deserve, then we're truly sorry we hurt Him. We see that sin is a killer. It's deadly. It's poisonous and we grow to hate it.

That's the kind of repentance for which God is looking–a true turning away from sin. The Bible says it's not just confessing our sins, but "whoever confesses and forsakes them (his sin), will have mercy" (Proverbs 28:13).

STEP 4

TO CONFESS

"I dwell in the midst of a people
of unclean lips."
Isaiah 6:5

Days of our Lives

Why does God want us to confess our sins, anyway? When I was a baby Christian, I used to have the idea that when I confessed my sins to God, I would say, "God, we need to have a talk. You better sit down now. There's some things I have to tell You," as though I was informing Him. I forgot that God knows everything!

But if God knows everything, then why do we need to confess? We also might ask, "If God knows everything, why pray?" Jesus tells us He knows the things we need before we even ask (Matthew 6:8). But He still tells us to ask. In the same way, He knows what our sins are before we confess. But He still wants us to confess them.

There are several reasons why God tells us to

41

do this. For one thing, it's simply polite. Our sins are against God. When we hurt a person, we should tell him or her we are sorry. Every time we sin, we hurt ourselves, we hurt others, and we hurt God. And so we are saying, "God, I'm sorry." Even though He knows that we have hurt Him, and we know that He knows, it's only proper to apologize.

Another reason is that it's God's method–God's plan for removing the guilt. It helps us to feel and believe we are forgiven. I think some people have never felt the freedom and peace that God wants us to enjoy as Christians because their confession is so shallow and brief. In many cases, we spend twenty, thirty or forty years sinning daily and hourly, offending our heavenly Father and then in a casual moment, we say, "Lord, forgive my sins." Somehow, we expect to find solace and relief from that shallow, shabby confession.

Now, I'm not saying that we should specifically confess every sin that we've ever committed. Nobody can remember everything he or she has done wrong, but we should be more specific. How specific? Some people can't even remember everything they've done wrong in one day!

But here's what I recommend, and it does work. I don't remember every lie that I have ever told, but I know that I was a liar. I don't remember every article that I have stolen, but I know I was a thief. So when it comes time to confess, I suggest that you take a piece of paper and write down, *I'm a thief, I'm a liar.* Write down, *impure thoughts, jealousy,* or whatever the sins might be. If you are afraid you are forgetting something, don't worry, if you ask God, the Holy Spirit will bring those things to your remembrance. You may be surprised at the length of the list!

One of the advantages to this kind of specific confession is that you are admitting that your sins are sins. In other words, it's easy enough to say, "Lord, I'm a sinner," but when you finally say, "Lord, I'm a gossip," it could be the first time you have acknowledged gossip as a sin. This allows the Holy Spirit to change you in that area.

After you've complied your list of categories of sins, start thinking of specific ones under each category. Again, if you ask, the Holy Spirit will bring to your mind the ones He knows you most need to confess. As you remember them, write them down under their categories.

After you have complied your list of things you need to confess to the Lord, kneel down and say, "Father, I am confessing my sins. I am guilty of these things." Then read your list to God. I know it may be painful, but it's extremely healthy for your soul! Then finish your prayer by saying, "Please forgive me, for Christ's sake."

We have the promise that, "if we confess our sins, He is faithful and just to forgive us our sins," and He will provide power, "to cleanse us from all unrighteousness" (1 John 1:9). That means freedom not only from the *penalty* of sin, which is death, but from the *power* of sin. When you do this, God will give you power to do right, to improve in these specific areas (1Corinthians 10:13). After you have confessed your sins, take the list and set it on fire or tie it to a rock and throw it in the ocean (Micah 7:19). (Perhaps shredding it would be more environmentally safe.)

Then there are some things you may need to confess to other people. For instance, if you have stolen something from someone, you should tell that person, and then, as far as possible, you should work to repay it (Ezek 33:15). If you have hurt a person, you must tell him or her you are sorry and try to reconcile the relationship.

I remember one time, when I was about fourteen years old and living in Florida with my father, I worked for Baskin-Robbins Ice Cream. My employer told me I could eat all the ice cream I wanted. He said I would get tired of it soon. He was wrong! After working there for a few weeks, I won his confidence. Because of the time I spent in military school, I was pretty good at being punctual and keeping things neat and clean. I opened and closed the store on time.

Eventually, he gave me the key to the cash register and showed me how to lock up the money each night. I am ashamed to say that one of the last times I ran away from home, I robbed from my employer. Although it wasn't very much—I only took $10. This haunted me for years because Mr. Scott had trusted me.

On one of my trips back to Miami Beach, I knew I needed to go back to Mr. Scott and tell him I had stolen from him, and repay the $10. I admit, I was pretty frightened as I walked up the street toward the 31 Flavors sign. I was wondering what he would think of my stealing after he had trusted me so much.

When I walked into the store, I asked the person behind the counter if I could speak with Mr. Scott. He looked at me with a puzzled expression and explained that Lee Scott had sold the store to them a couple of years earlier and moved. They had no idea how to locate him.

Suddenly, at that moment, I felt a great relief and burden lift from my shoulders. It wasn't the $10 that God was concerned about. I think the Lord was concerned whether I was willing to do His will. Was I willing to confess and pay back what I had done? He now knew I was.

Very few sins should be confessed publicly. There's a story, more like a parable, of a home Bible study during which one of the deacons from the church began to sob. When folks asked what the problem was, he said he couldn't hide his sin any longer. He said, "I feel like a hypocrite. I just have to let somebody know that I'm living a life of sin. I have been sleeping with the elder's wife."

The shocked people began to console and pray for the deacon that God would grant him victory.

Someone else who had been moved and touched by the deacon's openness also began to sob, and said, "I, too, think I should confess something. I don't know how to tell you this but I am a kleptomaniac. Everywhere I go, even though I hold a position in the church, I'm always stealing little things. Nothing big, but I always steal something."

One by one, just about every member of the Bible study began to confess a variety of different sins, many of them shocking and shameful things. Finally, everybody in the room except for one person had opened their soul and confessed some great secret sin.

Naturally, the other individuals in the Bible study began to look at this person who was sitting quietly in the corner. They said, "Brother, we've all been praying for one another and confessing our faults to one another. Isn't there something that you'd like to share?"

He said, "I, too, have a sin, but it's too wicked. I can't tell you what it is."

"Come now," they insisted, "what could be worse than all these awful things you've heard us share?" "No," he said, "it's just too dreadful. I'm afraid I can't!"

They gathered around and put their arms on his shoulder and said, "Don't you think you can trust us after everything we have told you? We've shared all this confidential information with you. Don't you think you can tell us what your problem is and know that it's safe with us? We know God will forgive you."

He finally said, "OK, if I must. My sin is gossip, and I can't wait to get out of here and tell everybody what I've heard tonight!"

I know that's a humorous anecdote, but it does have a point. Sometimes it can do more harm than good when we confess to others.

A sin that was committed publicly should be

publicly confessed. But the majority of the sins we commit are sins against God and should be confessed only to Him.

The most convincing way to tell the world that Jesus has forgiven your sins and given you a new heart is not with your talking, but with your walking!

Unbearable Problems

I had been living in the remote mountains outside of Covelo for sometime, and for 15 years Herman had been a thorn in my side. I had heard when the rangers at some of the State parks in California encounter bears that are aggressive and destructive with the campers, they avoid killing them. Instead, they trap these problem bears and ship them to remote parts of Northern California where they hope they won't be a threat to anyone.

I was living close to the Mendocino National Forest where they release some of these "troublesome" bears. The best I can figure is that Herman was among the problem bears from one of the State parks. He did not act like a typical wild bear.

When I first met Herman near my home years ago, he was in his prime. By the time this story happened, he must have been nearing retirement. I understand a black bear can live up to thirty years.

Early one morning I heard a terrific bang and our whole cabin shook. Then our goat Libby began to bleat desperately. Herman had snatched our 80 pound goat from under the house and was running up the hill. At that time I had been keeping my .22 rifle out in the truck. I must confess that I wasn't as brave as David in the Bible who put his life on the line to save a lamb from a bear. I wasn't ready to go out in the dark and chase down a hungry 400-pound black bear with at .22 rifle to rescue a goat! (Maybe for a sheep but not for a goat!) Shooting a black bear with a .22 is like putting out a fire with gasoline. It just infuriates the bear.

So that's how it went for many years. During that time, Herman tore up my fruit trees and stole goats. My dog, Prince, stopped staying at my home because Herman was eating his dog food and chased him away! At one point, he broke through the kitchen window and attempted to come inside. However, a friend who was staying in the house managed to scare him away by shooting a gun in the air. I even called my home owners insurance agent to find out if my house was covered in the event of bear attack. He said, "NO!" I knew that if I didn't do something soon, things would just get worse.

Some of the old-timers told me that a bear could do a lot of damage if he got into the house and started helping himself around the kitchen. "They don't just look in the cupboards," my friend said, "They tear the doors off the hinges and they never go out the same window they came in!"

Jesus tells us He stands at the door knocking, asking to come in (Revelation 3:20). He wants to abide in our lives, live in our hearts. Jesus always knocks. He waits patiently to be invited in. The devil doesn't have such good manners. He'll barge right in and ransack our hearts uninvited. Like a bear in the kitchen, he will tear your life apart. The only way to get him out of your heart is to let Jesus come in! Jesus is our ammunition. David killed Goliath with a rock and Jesus is the "Rock of ages" (1 Corinthians 10:4).

I knew I had to deal with Herman, but I was not a hunter. I don't even eat meat. I love animals and the thought of shooting a bear just wasn't very pleasant. I called the Forest Service and asked them what to do about my problem. After talking to them for a while, I got the distinct impression they were swamped with complaints about bears and probably could not do anything for a long time. They said they needed evidence, pictures and forms filled out. I knew if anything was going to happen, I would have to do it.

Every time I came back from an evangelistic meeting, I saw more evidence that Herman was getting ready to make his move and tear the house apart. One night I noticed claw marks on the side of my house. Some of the old hunters said that bears mark their territory in the woods by clawing trees. Herman had gone too far now. He had marked my home as his territory.

I went to a friend who is a hunter and with reluctance, I borrowed his elephant gun. You have to understand that this gun was about as big as a gun gets. It wasn't made by Winchester, Remington or Browning. It was actually made by a company that manufactures artillery! I fired it a few times just to see if I could get used to it. The sound from the explosion was like a sonic boom and the kickback nearly dislocated my shoulder.

I figured that I had made adequate preparation to deal with the problem, but I was still, quite frankly, afraid. For one thing, Herman was as big as a black bear gets! Secondly, I had never been bear hunting before.

Some of my friends made matters worse by reminding me of all the horror stories they'd heard. A wounded bear can be vicious and violent. But I kept reminding myself that if I didn't do something about Herman, he would soon destroy my home.

This is an illustration of how we often face the problems of sin in our lives. We know we must deal with them, but it's easier to put them off. We have all the answers. We've got the Scriptures. But we keep putting off doing anything because we're afraid of the battle and what might be involved in a conflict with the enemy.

But back to Herman. Finally, one cold fall night very late, I came home alone from an evangelistic meeting. Sure enough, I saw new evidence on the back porch that Herman had just been there. Not only were there fresh claw marks on the house, but I could see wet paw marks where he had just been eating Prince's dog food. My very cowardly canine had been scared off and was nowhere in sight.

I went upstairs to bed. I'll admit I didn't rest very well, because I knew Herman would be back.

Sure enough, early in the morning I heard crunching and rumbling downstairs. Is that Herman, I thought, or did Prince come back for breakfast?

I tiptoed downstairs unarmed in my red long johns and peeked out the kitchen window to the back porch. Even though the kitchen window is about four feet above the back porch, I saw this huge black bear looming like a mountain over the dog food dish. He was moving back and forth as he gobbled up the dog's food.

When I saw Herman on my porch, I thought to myself, "He's not hurting anything. Just let him eat the dog's food and he'll go away." But I knew that one of these days he would try to come into the house, so I'd better deal with him now.

Nowhere does the Bible say we are to look for a better time or a future day to come to the Lord and do battle with the devil. As soon as we see the problem, that's when God tells us to deal with it. The Bible says, "Now is the accepted time" (2 Corinthians 6:2).

My heart began to pound in my chest and the adrenaline began to race through my veins. I ran up stairs, took the elephant gun off the rack and started back down. I stood there for a long moment, staring at the kitchen door, knowing that Herman—400 pounds of hungry bear—was on the other side. I knew bears don't like to be interrupted while they are eating , so I thought to myself, "If I open the door and shoot Herman right there and if I kill him, I would have his blood all over the back porch. If I don't kill him, he'd have my blood all over the kitchen floor!" (I may have lived in a cave, but I'm very neat!)

At that point, I would like to think the Lord inspired me with a safer plan. Whenever Herman came and went from my house, he took a little trail. From a small window halfway up the stairs at the back of the house, I could see this trail. I ran up the stairs gun in hand, opened the window and removed the screen. Then I went back downstairs and did my best to scare Herman off the porch by stomping on the kitchen floor. It took a little jumping up and down to get his attention, but he eventually lumbered off the porch and up the trail behind the house. There he stopped to look back toward the dog's food.

This was the moment! The time had come. I ran back up the stairs and looked out the window. There he stood, a fine old bear. He looked like a black horse standing broadside about fifty yards away. Then suddenly it occurred to me that I didn't remember whether the gun was loaded. This was a fine time to think about that!

In the same way, friends, it's a big mistake to think that we can go up against the devil in times of temptation without first storing away the ammunition of God's Word in our minds. All the times that Jesus was tempted, He met every temptation with "It is written...It is written...It is written" (Matthew 4:4,7,10). If we expect to overcome the devil in the battles of life, we need to be fortifying our minds with God's truth. King David said, "Your Word I have hidden in my heart, that I might not sin against You" (Psalm 119:11).

So I opened up the bolt of the rifle to see if I had remembered to put a shell in the chamber. Sure enough, there it was. Then I tried to remember, was the safety on or off? There was a little switch on the gun, but I couldn't recall if forward or backward was the on position. The only way to test it was to pull the trigger. These thoughts were racing through my mind at supersonic speed. I knew I did not have time to linger long, because I had to deal with the problem.

I leveled the gun, aimed and squeezed the trigger. It seemed for a moment that time stood still. Then I heard this incredible sonic boom and felt the shock of the blast. Herman whirled around and headed for the woods at the same time that the recoil of the gun nearly threw me down the stairs.

When I recovered, I looked out the window to see if there was any evidence of a wounded bear, but he was gone. I decided it was time to put on some clothes and go scouting into the woods for Herman. If I was going to be found mauled by a wounded bear, it wasn't going to be in red long johns!

Dressing quickly, I went to the spot where Herman had been standing and saw the evidence that he had been hit. There was blood everywhere. "Now," I thought, "I may have a wounded bear on my hands." I could not let a wounded bear run around in the mountains because there were other families with children living nearby.

Again, I felt like I needed to check to see that the gun was loaded. I want to tell you this was one of the most frightening experiences of my life! My dog was gone, no one else was around and I had to go off tromping through the woods looking for a wounded 400 pound bear alone!

Finding Herman wasn't very hard. After only about fifty yards of following a trail of blood, I saw him lying in a black heap, motionless.

I went back to the house to call my friend. He quickly came to help me deal with the bear. With the help of a backhoe, we gave Herman a proper burial. We discovered that my aim had been perfect–one shot through the heart. But Herman was so tenacious that he was still able to run fifty yards. (I must confess, though, that I was aiming for his head!)

Once I had dealt with the problem. I felt so relieved knowing that I didn't have to continue living forever in fear. Now I could come home in peace and not worry about my house being torn apart.

We find heaven the same way. Jesus has left us a blood-stained path. When we have problems or habits and sin in our life that we put off dealing with, we can't have peace. We can't keep ignoring them. You have to load your gun for bear and fight some battles. But remember, with God's Word as ammunition, you will never lose.

TO RECEIVE GOD

*"Your iniquity is taken away,
and your sin is purged."*
Isaiah 6:7

Anyone Thirsty?

Many years ago a ship went down one night in the Atlantic Ocean east of South America. Three or four of the sailors were able to salvage a small lifeboat and they survived the first disaster but they drifted for several days at sea. They were able to sustain life for a little while by catching fish that were following the boat. But after only a couple of days, they began to suffer severely for lack of water. It's interesting that the human body cannot live without salt. And it cannot live without water. But if you drink saltwater, you will die.

After nearly four days of floating around in the ocean, the only water they had came from catching some drops in their shirts from a small cloudburst, then wringing the raindrops out into their mouths.

Finally they were spotted by another ship and rescued. When the captain on the rescuing vessel asked why they were so thirsty, they responded, "Because we had nothing to drink." The captain said, "Nothing to drink? You're in an ocean of fresh water!"

You see, evidently their boat had drifted to a part of the sea where the mighty Amazon River pushes fresh water over a hundred miles out into the Atlantic Ocean. These men had been floating in a sea of fresh water. They were so sure the water was salty that they didn't even try to drink it. All they would have had to do was to reach over the side of the boat to get all the water they needed. They were dying of thirst while floating in life saving water!

Jesus said, "Whoever desires, let him take the water of life freely" (Revelation 22:17). Yet the world is dying from spiritual thirst while floating in a sea of living water!

I remember when I was living up in the cave, the first time I chose to give my life to the Lord, the devil said, "What are you doing praying like this? God won't forgive you. You've been too wicked."

But I reasoned, "What have I got to lose? I might as well try it. I've tried everything else." So I reached out and up and He took my hand. God is never very far away!

It's like the woman who came home from work to discover that she had left her house key at the office. Knowing the upstairs bathroom window was open, she climbed up on the roof via a nearby wall and tried to squeeze through the small window. But she was only able to get halfway in, and then became hopelessly stuck. She could not get in, nor could she get out. The neighbors heard her cries for help and called the fire department. The firemen and police arrived, not to mention the local newsmen and all the area neighbors. They came to look at her posterior and legs dangling out the window flaying into empty space.

She was quickly rescued when a fireman entered the house and pulled her inside. After she had dusted herself off, blushing she asked the fireman how he got into the house.

"I walked through the front door," he said. "Evidently it had been unlocked the whole time." She never even reached out and tried it!

I wonder why so many people are so reluctant to exercise a little faith and reach out to God. Even if our faith is small, we need to give God a chance! The Bible says that as soon as we draw near to God, He draws near to us (James 4:8).

"Blessed are those who hunger and thirst for righteousness, for they shall be filled" (Matthew 5:6).

Falcon

In our story of Isaiah's conversion, we see that God sometimes needs to use heat to melt our stony hearts and enable us to receive His forgiveness and cleansing. In the Bible this heat or fire represents the trials and suffering God allows us to encounter in order to teach us lessons of faith.

I have one brother–or perhaps I should say I had one brother. You see, not too long ago my brother, Falcon, passed away. He was born with a terminal disease called cystic fibrosis. This disease affects the lungs. Even though the average life expectancy is between 15 to 18 years, through some persistence he learned or inherited and the grace of God, he lived to be 35 years old.

His typical day consisted of waking up and coughing. He took pills by the handful, sometimes without water because he had become so accustomed to it. Then he would receive respiratory therapy so he could continue breathing. He spent the rest of his day doing exercises and inhaling mist simply to keep breathing. It was like fighting off drowning all day long.

Falcon was a tremendous individual. He started a camp for kids with CF and was always concerned about other people's needs. Part of the reason for his sensitivity to the hurts and needs of others was that he had suffered so much during his life. The trials of his disease taught him to love.

One time when I was in Florida, Falcon and I were out jogging together. After running 100 yards he stopped to have a coughing fit. When he had regained his composure, we walked for a while.

"Doug," he said, "you're lucky." I wondered exactly what he meant. I had dropped out of school and run away, while Falcon finished college and worked for Dad. He had a new house right on the water in Miami Beach, three new cars and a boat.

"What do you mean, Falcon?" I asked as we stopped walking so he could catch his breath again.

He said, "I'd give everything I own to have your lungs."

And I would have given him my lungs if I could! There was a hidden message in his words that day. He was saying that there is nothing more important than life. He was willing to sacrifice every earthly belonging or position for even a little more of this life.

Yet, we Christians are sometimes so reluctant to deny ourselves a habit or practice for Jesus and *everlasting* life. "For what is a man profited if he shall gain the whole world, and lose his own soul?" (Matthew 16:26).

Because Falcon had seen so much hypocrisy in the name of Christianity, he had a hard time accepting religion per se. He would always say exactly what was on his mind. Often he would gently tease me when I offered to pray as we ate together.

One day I received a phone call from the family that Falcon had been admitted to the hospital and would probably not come home. I quickly took a plane to Florida, praying all the way that I would be able to see my brother before he died. I wanted to at least be able to tell him again that I loved him. And I wanted to pray with him.

My family is not at all religious. Some of them profess to be either agnostic or atheist. Falcon at least accepted that there was a God. He just had trouble believing in any organized religion.

When I arrived in Florida, my father met me and we went straight to the hospital. My brother was sitting up in bed, leaning over one of those rolling hospital tables, lying with his chest on a pillow, struggling to breathe. He had been sitting in this position for the last two days. He knew if he lay down he would no longer be able to breathe. The doctor told us that just a fraction of one of his lungs was still working. He had an oxygen mask on with the oxygen turned up all the way. When my father and I came into the room, he opened his eyes and nodded.

For a long time I just sat there holding his hand. I must confess that it was a very tense moment. My mother and father had gone through a bitter divorce thirty years earlier and now they had to be in the same room because of their common love for Falcon.

In the same way I have seen that out of a common love for Jesus, Christians can learn to put aside differences and get along with each other. The disciples of Jesus were angry with each other, vying for the highest position until they saw Jesus on the cross for their sins. Next we see them praying together in one accord (Luke 22:24; Acts 2:1).

Falcon married a wonderful woman. Even though he had a terminal disease, the Lord gave him a very supportive wife. From time to time when I came to Florida to visit, Sandy would go to church with me. She has probably been the one in the family who has respected my religion and values as a Christian more than anyone else. The rest of my family has sometimes hinted that I am wasting my life in the ministry. Some of them have chided me for not coming to work with my Dad and helping him with his business. I'll confess that at times I have been tempted to do this. I just wanted to be with my father and to be able to work with him. But I know the Lord has called me to do something different.

After being at the hospital for a while, Sandy asked my brother if it would be okay if I prayed. This was the first time my family had ever asked me to pray. Falcon couldn't speak because he had an oxygen mask on, but he nodded, yes.

It had never been so hard or so important for me to pray before. I prayed one of the most intense prayers of my life. I remember that I prayed for the Lord to be with Falcon, for him to have peace in his heart and his body and to be with the family and for His will to be done.

I sensed that God's Spirit had come into the room. My mother, who was a very strong individual, began to sob and cry. Sandy was crying. Falcon was squeezing my hand. Suddenly I knew they all realized through this trial we were experiencing, that God is ultimately the only answer for the needs in our lives.

Not long after I prayed, Falcon asked if he could lie down. After sitting up to keep breathing for two days, I knew he had resigned himself that it was now time to die. I sensed that he must have felt some peace with God in his heart after we prayed together. He couldn't talk to us because he had a mask on his face, so we helped him recline in the bed. He gave me a couple of hand signals to raise his head, then lower the bed. Then he gave me a very deliberate "okay" sign to say he finally felt a position where he could breathe at least a little bit.

With the family out of the room, I sat down next to Falcon and I said, I'll just talk to you," and he nodded. I told him a little about my children. He never had any of his own and he was always deeply interested in how they were doing. I didn't feel it was important to get him to say a little speech or to utter some words or to have some kind of last rites. I just wanted to be with him and to let him know that I loved him. I felt peace in my heart that he would be in the kingdom and that he had put his trust in the Lord.

Falcon's breathing grew slower and slower and I knew that he would die soon. I called Sandy and my mother back into the room and we all held his hand. Within a few minutes he breathed his last breath.

Even though the family knew he had a terminal disease, nobody had made any preparation for his funeral. No one wants to think they will die or that anyone they love will die. But suddenly everyone in the family realized there was a need for a minister. They asked if I would take charge of the service and make the arrangements. I was thankful for the opportunity because when you are grieving, you need to do something. It was through this fiery trial of watching a loved one die, that everyone realized their need of God and the importance of spiritual things.

We all have a terminal disease. Life is terminal. Sin is the disease. Even though Jesus can forgive us, we will all die the first death unless He comes first, so we should make preparation now.

Because Falcon knew his life was terminal, he worked hard to take care of his body. He valued every moment and lived life to the fullest. If we remember that this life is short and uncertain, we will cherish every moment and be more faithful to seek first God's kingdom.

God does not allow trials to come upon just bad or unconverted people. Bad things happen to good people as well. Remember Job's suffering, and Joseph who spent several years in prison as God prepared him for his lifework. The apostles, and of course, Jesus, suffered for doing good.

You will notice that after Isaiah confessed his sin was unclean lips, God placed coal on that specific place. All of us have different sins and different temptations. We are all sinners, but each of our sins are different. Some people have comforted themselves that because they do not kill, rape or steal, they are "little" sinners. In God's eyes, there's no such thing as a "little" sinner. We are all "big" sinners. The reason we know we are "big" sinners is that we all need a "big" Savior who has offered "big" forgiveness. All of us, regardless of how minuscule we may think our faults are, have committed sins that are titanic enough by themselves to put Jesus on the cross!

Isaiah said, "Woe is me," because he was a man of unclean lips. Though some church members may flatter themselves that they have never committed serious sins like murder, adultery, or theft, God tells us that anger in our hearts toward someone else is one of the most offensive sins. Thus backbiting and gossip are murder, too. The Lord considers these sins every bit as serious as any others.

Some of us say, "Yes, I love my neighbor," but then we spend a great deal of time talking about the faults of others (James 3:5-10).

We need to confess, "Lord, I'm a man of unclean lips." We need to ask God to put the coal wherever He sees it is needed.

You also notice that God uses hot coals to purify His people. The Scripture tells us that God is coming for a church that is without spot or wrinkle (Ephesians 5:27). The way you get out most spots is with hot water. And the way you get out the wrinkles is with a hot iron.

Many Christians are surprised when the Lord allows them to go through fiery trials to purify their faith and refine their characters, but the heat is God's blessed method of purifying His people. So remember, it may take a heavy load to bring you to your knees. God may have to put you flat on your back before you look up. And though you may feel at times like a useless lump of black coal, with a little heat and pressure, God will turn you into a diamond!

"Beloved, think it not strange concerning the fiery trial which is to try you, as though some strange thing happened unto you: But rejoice, inasmuch as ye are partakers of Christ's sufferings; that, when his glory shall be revealed, ye may be glad also with exceeding joy" (1 Peter 4:12, 13).

TO HEAR GOD

"Also I heard the voice of the Lord, saying. . .
Isaiah 6:8

Don't Fly With Feelings

A few years back I was doing an evangelistic series in Anderson, California. During that time, John Lomacang, my singing evangelist, his wife, Angie, and I were invited to go to Crescent City and speak in preparation for a series of meetings we would soon be starting there. The problem was that Anderson and Crescent City are 235 miles apart, with a crooked, two-lane road between them. I could not drive there in the morning and get back the same evening in time to continue our meetings in Anderson.

Since I am a pilot, I thought the best solution would be to fly. So I rented a plane in Redding and early the next morning, John, Angie, and I arrived at the airport. I called Crescent City to make sure the airport was open and clear. It was, so we took off.

Perhaps I should explain that John and Angie both had a terrific fear of flying, especially John. He was even afraid of flying in a 747, jumbo jet let alone in a single engine airplane! (I'm glad to let you know they are both flying all over the world now) I assured them, that they had nothing to worry about and with some reluctance they climbed into the plane.

As we flew along, I did everything I could to reassure them. It was, after all, a beautiful day and a smooth flight. But as we approached the coast where Crescent City was supposed to be, I discovered that the fog had rolled in from the ocean and I could not see the airport. In fact, the entire town had disappeared under a blanket of fluffy white. All we saw were hundreds of miles of mountains that disappeared into a sea of white fog. Then, to my dismay, I discovered the radio instruments at the Crescent City airport were not operating.

I should add that the area between Redding and Crescent City is the largest untouched wilderness still left in California. For hundreds of square miles in any direction, there's nothing but forest and mountains.

I remembered that Crescent City was at the end of a river, so I went up and down the coast, following the fog line looking for a river. However, I flew around in circles so long trying to decide what to do that I lost track of where I was. I finally found a river and thought if I could follow the river by flying underneath this ceiling of fog, then I could soon find Crescent City and the airport. Getting out later would be no problem. I would just fly straight up and after a few hundred feet of white we would break into the open blue.

I tried to act cheerful and unconcerned as I lowered the plane under the ceiling of fog and began to follow the river with mountains on both sides. It was something like flying through a tunnel.

We flew along, following the river, till we got to where I thought Crescent City was supposed to be, but instead there was a sea underneath us. The river had tuned into the Pacific Ocean! We were on our way to Japan. As much as I would have enjoyed seeing Japan, I knew I did not have enough fuel, and besides, I was supposed to be doing something else that morning!

I wondered how John and Angie were reacting to some of these changes in plans, so I looked back and saw that Angie was sleeping peacefully. I commented to John, "I'm glad to see your wife is able to relax and sleep."

He quickly responded, "She's not relaxed. She fainted!"

At this point I didn't know where the mountains were. I thought I had better just fly straight up and break through the fog and head back toward the coast. I was not instrument rated, but in order to get your pilot's license you need to have some training in flying by your instruments.

When you pull up into the fog, you lose all sense of bearing, because you have nothing visible by which to gauge your attitude of flight. As a matter of fact, I have heard stories of pilots who flew into a cloud, and when they came out the other side, they were flying completely upside down! When you are flying at 120 miles per hour in a cloud, it's hard for your body to judge your relation to the ground and angle and at which you are traveling.

As we flew through the clouds for a few moments, I thought we were heading straight up and level, but when I looked at my instruments, they said I was now going down and turning. I looked at John. He didn't look any more concerned than usual and it didn't feel like we were going down and turning. I'll confess it was a profound struggle to make the decision to follow my instruments instead of my feelings. Everything in my body told me that we were going up and level, but my instruments said we were going down and turning. I had to choose whether to follow my instruments or to follow my feelings.

One thing I learned in my flight instruction was never to fly by my feelings. "Trust your instruments," the instructor said over and over. So, ignoring everything I felt, I began to turn the plane in order to level my instruments. Then I pulled back on the stick and added power so that the instruments said we were going up and level.

Now John, and Angie who had recovered, were looking at me wondering what I was doing. "Why are you turning?" John asked. I explained to them that I had to follow my instruments. And it was a good thing I did, because after a few more minutes of fighting my feelings and following the instrument panel, we broke through the fog into the blue sky and I discovered that the instruments were correct. I also noticed a range of steep daunting mountains just off to the left where I had been turning! If I had not followed my instruments, we certainly would have crashed into a mountain or the ocean.

So it is in the Christian life. The Bible is the only safe guide to follow. We cannot trust our feelings. It's never safe to make spiritual decisions that are based only on how you feel. Feelings can be governed by a number of variables–what you've eaten, the condition of your health, or even the weather. All these things can change, but the Word of God is like a rock. It's a solid anchor that never moves or changes.

Our decisions must be based on what the Word says, not what everyone around us is saying. Even the norms and traditions of the church that have been accepted for many years are not a trustworthy guide. The Bible says there are many things that are highly esteemed by people but are an abomination to God (Luke 16:15). If you follow your feelings and if you follow the crowd, you will crash. It's not even safe to follow a religious crowd. Remember, it was a religious crowd that crucified Jesus.

One query that I frequently hear from new Christians is how do you know whose interpretation of the Bible to follow? Every church teaches something a little different.

I sincerely believe that the biggest battle we

face in understanding God's Word is simply being willing to do what it says. If we are honestly and sincerely wanting to do whatever God says, then it is God's responsibility to help us know what He wants us to do. We need not only a willingness to do God's will, but Jesus says we also need to be willing to seek to know His will, to ask, and to knock. And we should not knock just once or twice. Sometimes we need to knock until our knuckles are numb!

The Bible says, "You will seek Me and find Me, when you search for Me with all your heart" (Jeremiah 29:13). That is probably the most important commandment in the Christian life!

Some might say, "But I still have trouble understanding the Bible."

The secret to hearing and understanding God's voice is being committed and listening. You see, when a person is a born-again Christian, when he's been cleansed, then he'll hear God's voice. He may not understand at first, but the more he listens, the more he will understand.

It's like an infant. The parents lean over the crib and talk to their baby and say things like, "Mommy and Daddy love you." "Are you hungry?" The baby at first doesn't understand what in the world his parents are saying, but he knows that they love him. The more he listens and the more he grows, the more he understands. As baby Christians, we may not understand everything in God's Word, but we understand the basics and the more we listen and read, the more we understand.

When I read the Bible I found in my cave, there was a lot I didn't understand. But after reading the Gospels, I understood that God loved me. I understood that I was a big sinner and He was a big Savior. And that was a good starting point. From there on, as I continued reading, I understood His voice better, and I began to better understand His will. Sometimes we have trouble understanding what God is saying because we're not willing to listen to His voice.

A young lady attended a series of evangelistic meetings I was conducting. Night after night I could see her eyes brighten and she was sitting on the edge of her seat. She seemed to be drinking in God's Word with great enthusiasm. But about three-quarters of the way through the series, I noticed a sudden change. She sat back in her seat with her arms folded and her eyebrows knit together. I knew something was wrong.

So I went to visit her. When I asked how she was enjoying the meetings, she said, "For the first few weeks it was tremendous. I could hear the Lord speaking to me. I was opening the Bible, and I could understand what God was saying, but then you covered a subject that I just didn't appreciate."

As we talked I discovered that God's Word went against a practice in her life that she knew she needed to change and she had no intention of changing. So she put on the brakes. She told me that it seemed now she was not getting anything out of the meetings and when she read the Bible it just looked like back ink on white paper.

I said, "Could it be that God is not speaking to you because you're not listening to Him?"

Being a Christian is a series of progressive steps. As long as we're willing to listen, God is willing to speak. The Bible says that if we turn away our ear from hearing the law, then even our prayers become an abomination (Proverbs 28:9). If we stubbornly stop listening to God, He'll ultimately stop speaking to us. If there are some areas in our life where we are plugging our ears and turning our heads, then the Lord cannot reveal new things and direct our paths.

Humble Pie

The Lord speaks to us in a variety of ways. Primarily, He speaks to us through the Scriptures, but He also communicates to us through Christian ministers, Christian books, nature and providence.

The Bible tells of the night Peter saw Jesus walking on the water and Jesus invited him to walk on the water, too (Matthew 14:28, 29). When Peter stepped out of the boat and into the stormy waves, as long as he kept his eyes on Jesus, he was easily able to rise above the tempest around him and do the impossible, walk on water! But then he became proud. He took his eyes off of Jesus to see if his friends were watching him, and he began to go down. The Bible says that when he saw the waves, his faith began to sink, and when his faith began to sink, he began to sink, too.

Then Peter said a very short prayer: "Lord, save me" (Matthew 14:30)!

According to Mark, as soon as Peter acknowledged his mistake and asked for help, Jesus stretched out His hand and helped him up. And as soon as Isaiah confessed and repented, the Lord sent cleansing and forgiveness (Isaiah 6:7).

Every human being is on probation, but that doesn't mean we're on trial to prove ourselves. You see, as soon as we sincerely repent and confess our sins, God immediately offers cleansing, forgiveness, and power to live a different life.

You can be sure Peter never forgot this experience. It taught him two important lessons: (1) When you take your eyes off of Jesus, you start to sink in your stormy circumstances and (2) when you reach out to Jesus, you start to rise above the storm.

One of the first temptations a person falls into when he succeeds is pride. Early in my ministry, when I had just begun preaching, I met with a modest amount of success. I believed everything people said as they filed out of church after listening to a sermon. I have since learned to take these compliments with a grain of salt! Cordial praise is like perfume, sniff it but don't swallow it or it will make you sick. Sometimes people say these nice things at the door after a sermon because they don't know what else to say.

I was in the middle of a seminar, the church was packed, the people seemed to be very interested and I think I was becoming a little proud at my ability to hold an audience. On one such night, I was preaching my heart out. I felt that energy and eloquence for which ministers pray. The words were flowing easily, and I noticed that the congregation seemed to be captivated, sitting on the edge of their seats, their eyes open wide. I had their undivided attention!

After the closing prayer I hurried back to the main door, expecting to drink in a flood of compliments, words of approval and commendation. Instead, the very first person who came to the door was a middle-aged lady who rushed to me and whispered, "Doug, I wanted to hurry back. Someone needs to tell you that your zipper has been open all evening long, and I think everyone else will be afraid to say anything for fear of embarrassing you!"

My, my! Talk about a humiliating experience–talk about hearing the voice of the Lord through providence (Numbers 22:28)! God in His love gave me that incident of gentle rebuke to teach me a lesson I will never forget! I am reminded that God can use almost anyone. He can even speak through a donkey if He wants (Numbers 22:28)!

I have learned from that experience that God can work in our lives, and even when we get out of hand we still belong to Him. He promises to chasten us and bring us back or down, whatever the case may require.

Now when I'm preaching and it seems that people are listening and I have the audience's attention, I don't worry about getting proud–but I do worry about my pants!

STEP 7

TO GO FOR God

*"Then I said, **Here am I! Send me.**"*
Isaiah 6:8

Dead Sea or Galilee?

There are two principal bodies of water in
Palestine and though the same river feeds into both
seas they are vastly different. One, of course, is the Sea
of Galilee. The other is the Dead Sea.

The Jordan River runs into the Sea of Galilee from
north and out the south. It is full of life, even though for
thousands of years fishermen have fished those waters. The
secret to its constant, prolific life is that it has a regular fresh
supply of water running in one end and then back out the
other.

Just a few miles to the south is the lowest point
on planet earth. Thirteen hundred feet below sea level,
you will find the Dead Sea, a place where once stood
the wicked cities of Sodom and Gomorrah. It's called
the Dead Sea because it contains no life. There's not a

single fish or tadpole in that entire body of water.

The Jordan River runs into the Sea of Galilee and the Jordan River runs into the Dead Sea. One is full of life and one is full of death. What makes the difference?

The secret is that the Jordan River also runs out of the Sea of Galilee, but nothing runs out of the Dead Sea. Because it is a very warm desert region, the water evaporates faster than it can fill the basin and run out. Since the Dead Sea is always taking and never giving it has become stagnant and dead. It is a sink full of minerals and salts. Not a single pollywog, tadpole or minnow can survive in it.

The principle is the same in the Christian life. You cannot survive and thrive as a Christian unless you are sharing what the Lord imparts to others. This is true in almost every area of life. As we have one hand open before the Lord receiving, we must also have the other hand open to the world in giving.

A Christian cannot stay fresh unless he becomes a channel of blessings to others. If we take the gospel and the plan of salvation and then just forever roost on it in church and warm in the pew, our experience will dry up and die. I believe this is one of the reasons why such a high percentage of baby Christians expire. They're taught to accept the good news, but nobody involves them in sharing it.

A new Christian may say, "I don't know enough to share." Nobody knows everything. God asks us to share what we do know. Part of the Christian's growing process is sharing salvation. For years I always felt guilty when I found myself sharing Jesus, because I thought I wasn't worthy, there were still too many defects and faults in my character. How could God use me to bring the message of life to someone else when my character was so flawed?

But then I read a passage in the Bible where Jesus turned to Peter one day and said, "Satan has asked for you, that he may sift you as wheat. But I have prayed for you, that your faith should not fail; and when you have returned to Me, strengthen your brethren." Luke 22:31,32.

When are you converted? This was about three years into the ministry of Christ. Jesus had sent Peter and the other apostles on several preaching missions that were attended by miracles, and now Jesus says to Peter, "When you are converted."

You mean the Lord can use people who are not thoroughly converted? Yes, I think the Bible means just that. Part of our conversion process is in working for the Lord, in sharing what we do have.

Peter made a commitment to believe in Jesus and follow Him, but he had not been thoroughly converted. I don't know if there is anyone who is a Christian who would claim to be perfect. Though I believe preachers and laymen should practice what they preach. Sharing the gospel at every opportunity becomes part of our conversion process.

I pick up hitchhikers as a part of my personal witnessing. Over the course of my Christian life, I have picked up hundreds of hitchhikers and have had a variety of experiences, most of them good. A couple of reasons I do this are, I know how they feel having done a lot of hitchhiking in my past and I have a captive audience! I find it's very helpful to wait until I'm on an interstate highway going about sixty-five miles per hour before making my gospel presentation! Then, when I ask the person if they want to accept Jesus, I stare at them and accelerate. I get a lot more decisions that way. (Just kidding!)

I remember one experience when I was driving the winding Covelo road by myself. I had been having some personal trials and I began to feel sorry for myself. I think we all have days when we think we'll never make it as Christians, when we're ready to throw in the towel; we feel discouraged, as though there are too many changes we need to make.

I was in this depressed state of mind when I reached the turnoff for Highway 101. I saw a young man sitting on the roadside hitchhiking. With some degree of reluctance, I pulled over and picked him up. I questioned whether I was in any spiritual condition to help somebody else, but I probably have 50,000 miles on my thumb from hitchhiking and I know how it feels to sit there hour after hour hoping someone will give you a lift, so I pulled over.

When this young man got into my car, he was very thankful and animated and wanted to talk. When he found out that I was a minister, he came up with a whole list of questions. "What exactly is a Christian?" "What do you believe?" "What church do you go to?"

Little by little, as I attempted to answer his

questions, I felt myself emerging from my depression. By the time I dropped him off twelve miles down the road, I was praising the Lord for the opportunity to share the good news, even in a small way, with another soul.

Sharing my faith was God's method of reminding me that He is real. This is one of the main reasons why I am involved in the ministry. Not only do I receive a blessing from seeing other people come to Christ, but I am kept alive by sharing the "good news" with them.

The Magic of Mercy

I know the Lord must have a sense of humor! There are some things that He says in His Word that seem to illustrate this. For instance, try to picture a man with a log in his eye pulling a speck out of a friend's eye. Or picture someone trying to lead a camel through the eye of a needle!

I remember one hot day as I was hitchhiking, I prayed earnestly for a ride in a car with air conditioning! Well, I got a ride in the back of a pickup truck, with plenty of air conditioning!

On another occasion, while I was driving alone from Texas to California pulling a trailer, I prayed that the Lord would give me someone to whom I could witness. I have prayed that prayer many times. It is a good way to occupy the hours. Nothing makes driving time pass more quickly for me than when I am sharing my faith with someone else.

Shortly after I prayed, I saw a young Hispanic gentleman with long black hair standing on the side of the road. He was dressed in what I thought was a peculiar fashion. The weather outside was below freezing, but he was only wearing tennis shoes, blue jeans and a white dress shirt.

I pulled over and he quickly jumped in. He was rubbing his hands together as he shivered and I could see he was very cold. I turned the heater in my old 1951 Chevy pickup on high to give him as much warmth as possible. It didn't take me long to assess the situation. Evidently he had recently come across the border somewhere near Deming, New Mexico and was trying to get a ride and find some work in the "Promised Land."

I tried to generate a conversation with him, but quickly discovered that he didn't speak a bit of English. About the only Spanish I knew was "si, uno, dos, tres. . .tostada, burrito and enchilada!" I thought to myself, "Lord, thanks a lot! Very funny! I asked for someone to witness to and he can't even understand me!"

I decided that if ever a person needed the gift of "tongues," I did right then. So I asked the Lord to help me communicate the gospel to this young man during the time we had together.

Through a series of miracles, I was able to understand that he was looking for work and somehow I managed to get across that I could give him some work, because I was selling firewood at that time. He was so excited! I don't think he had any idea that it would take three days of driving to get to my house.

I had never spoken Spanish before, but by the time we arrived in Northern California, I was able to speak enough Spanish to share the gospel with this young man! He came and lived with us for several months and helped me in the firewood business. He attended church and was eventually baptized. Just before his baptism, he stood up in the church and addressed the people. Through the help of a translator, he shared a gripping testimony in which he openly stated that when I picked him up, he had intended to rob and kill me because he could see that I kept a bundle of cash in my jacket pocket. He had been a thief in Chihuahua City, Mexico and knew what to do.

He went on to explain that every time we stopped somewhere, I offered to buy him something to eat or something to drink and when I noticed he needed warmer clothing, I stopped and obtained it for him through a church charity. He summarized his testimony by stating that he really didn't want to murder me because I was being so kind and because I gave him everything he needed!

So kindness not only wins people to Christ, it can even save your life!

When Lot invited the angels into his house, he did it because he was concerned for their safety, never dreaming they were there to save his life (Genesis 19).

When Rebecca watered Abraham's camels, she never dreamed that by this little act of kindness she would be chosen as Isaac's wife (Genesis 24). Rahab was saved from death by showing kindness to the two spies. (Joshua 6:25) When the poor widow offered Elijah her last loaf of bread, she and her son didn't imagine they would be miraculously provided for during the rest of the famine (I Kings 17:11).

The two great commandments are to love God and love your neighbor (Matthew 22:36-10). The way we show our love for our neighbor is in deeds of mercy and kindness.

Many people never realize the vital role mercy and kindness will play in the judgment. Jesus will separate the saved from the lost based upon how they have loved their neighbors.

The Bible says: "Then the King will say to those on His right hand, 'Come, you blessed of My Father, inherit the kingdom prepared for you from the foundation of the world: for I was hungry and you gave Me food; I was thirsty and you gave Me drink; I was a stranger and you took Me in; I was naked and you clothed Me; I was sick and you visited Me; I was in prison and you came to Me.'

"Then the righteous will answer Him, saying, 'Lord, when did we see You hungry and feed You, or thirsty and give You drink? When did we see You a stranger and take You in, or naked and clothe You? Or when did we see You sick or in prison and come to You?'

"And the King will answer and say to them,

'Assuredly, I say to you, inasmuch as you did it to one of the least of these My brethren, you did it to Me.'"

(Matthew 25:34-40)

"He has shown you, O man, what is good; and what does the Lord require of you but to do justly, to love mercy and to walk humbly with your God."

(Micah 6:8)

Friends, did you catch the meaning of these passages? They tell us that the bottom line in the judgment is how we live our love! It's one thing to say, "I love the Lord and my neighbor," but it's another to demonstrate that love through deeds of kindness.

Jesus spent more time healing and feeding people than preaching to them. Those who experience His works of love are often the most ready to listen to His words of life.

Someone Needs to Tell Them

A mother in North Africa
   Struggles day by day.
Her children labor in the fields,
   They seldom laugh, they seldom play.

Their father's heart is heavy
   And his hands are sore.
The burden that he carries is not a lack of bread.
   He's wishing for this family something more.

There's a man in Georgia,
  Pushing eighty years.
His friends down at the coffee shop
  Don't see his pain, or lonely tears.

He has some children somewhere,
  So he lingers by the phone.
He's afraid of dying, but he's more afraid of life.
  Who will tell him he is not alone?

When Jesus rose victorious,
  He spoke His battle plan.
Go tell every nation,
  Every woman, every man.

The Great Commission challenge,
  Teach the old and young,
From your friends at hand to a foreign land,
  Every race and every tongue.

Someone needs to tell them,
  Someone needs to share,
Show them life eternal,
  and Jesus' love and care.

Someone needs to sacrifice
  And let the children know.
Someone needs to tell them,
  Someone needs to go.

Doug Batchelor

CONCLUSION

Pull the Plug

When I was about 14 years old, I lived with my father in Miami Beach, Florida. He had a house right on Biscayne Bay with a yacht, and also a small ski boat. From time to time Dad would trust me enough to let me take the motorboat out with my friends, but he always warned me not to leave the bay. "Don't take the boat out into the ocean," he would say.

As you have probably gathered, I wasn't always careful in my younger years to follow instructions. On one such occasion, I decided to disregard Dad's warning. I had a couple of buddies with me in the boat, and we headed through the bay underneath the bridge, and through the channel into the open sea. I wasn't prepared for the height of the waves out there, and as we tried to mount the waves and power our way through the strait and out into the open sea the boat started nosing into some of the larger swells, and soon water was swamping our little sixteen foot ski boat.

I could see the terror in my friends faces as I tried to turn the lumbering boat around and head it back into the bay. The boat was so full of water that I could barely get the steering to respond. It was like riding in a motorized Jacuzzi except the water was cold! My friends were grabbing frantically for anything they could use to bail the sea water out of the boat. One of them used a diving mask, the other a coffee can, but I knew at that rate it was like trying to drain a bathtub with a teaspoon.

As I tried to navigate back under the bridge into the bay, I called to one of my friends, "Pull the plug!"

All boats this size have a plug at the lower back that can be pulled to let the water out when the boat is on land.

My friend looked up at me in disbelief and said, "What?"

I yelled again, "Pull the plug! Pull the plug!"

He shouted, "We're already about to sink, and you want me to pull the plug?"

"Trust me!" I said. "Pull the plug!"

It took some doing to push aside the floating gas cans and debris and reach down through the knee-deep water to find the little plug in the back of the boat below the engine. When my friend found it, he looked at me one more time as if to say, "Are you sure this is what you want me to do?" I nodded my head, Yes!

As soon as he had pulled the plug, I pushed the engine throttle all the way forward, and as we began to accelerate, our momentum forced the water out through the hole in the back of the boat. Soon we were flying along through the calm bay with all the water drained out, at which time my friend replaced the plug.

When water begins to creep into your ship, the answer isn't to spend all your time bailing with a teaspoon. The answer is to pull the plug and give it the gas! If we get involved doing what Jesus has called us to do, our troubles will "run out" automatically.

As I visit various churches, I am saddened to discover that many members are so involved with the internal problems of the church, turning molehills into mountains and examining their own belly buttons, that the pastors are preoccupied with being referees and massaging the saints. Very little is done in these churches by way of outreach.

When I come to a church like that and start an evangelistic meeting, and on opening night the pews are filled with people from the community searching for something better, it's amazing to see the transformation that comes over the members.

Suddenly they begin to value what they have in Christ and Christianity. As they see the people coming night after night, soaking up and appreciating the gospel truths they have taken for granted for so long, it brings a revival into their hearts, too.

Jesus tells us that we are to be in the world, but

the world is not supposed to be in us (John 17:14-16). It's sort of like a boat out on the ocean. It's normal for a boat to be in the water. In fact, a boat looks kind of funny on dry land! The problem comes when the water gets in the boat.

I don't think external forces have ever been the greatest threat to the church. It's not the woodpeckers on the outside, but the termites on the inside that do the greatest damage.

Many years ago when Abraham Lincoln was first campaigning for President, he and a friend were riding through a southern county, and they came upon a town where some black slaves were being auctioned. In anger, Lincoln asked the coachman to stop the buggy, and he watched for a few moments. The hair stood up on the back of his neck as he witnessed the human cargo being bought and sold. He said to his friends, "I can't do anything about this right now, but someday I will, and when I hit it, I'm going to hit it hard."

That's the philosophy we should all have when we accept Christ and become Christians. If you are going to be a Christian, then be a Christian. Go for it with all your heart, all your mind, and all your soul. The Bible says, "Whatever your hand finds to do, do it with all your might" (Ecclesiastes 9:10).

You can't treat your Christian experience as if it were some kind of timid experiment. For instance, "I wonder whether this works? Or I think I'll try that for a while." You need to go for it with all your heart and soul. When David went out to fight Goliath, he didn't try to bring the giant down, he didn't wonder whether he could. The Bible says Goliath walked out to meet David, but David ran to meet the giant (1 Samuel 17:40). You must have faith and confidence that you can do what God tells you to do, and then go for it with all your heart. Do not put your hand to the plow while looking back, longing for the world (Luke 9:26).

Jesus tells us that all things are possible to them that believe (Mark 9:23). Our Christian experience will usually be a reflection of our faith. Our relationship to the Lord will be in proportion to how we believe in Him and how much we trust Him! Now don't misunderstand, in the battle with the enemy, faith is not the only available tool. In addition to faith, I believe God has given every person a free will, and we must not underestimate the power of the will. You've got to want to do something. You've got to have a desire.

Sometimes when I work with people to overcome a habit such as drinking or smoking, they say, "I just can't take it anymore. I have to have a cigarette."

So I ask, "How long do you think you could go without a cigarette if someone put a gun to your head and told you he'd pull the trigger if you lit up?"

They'll ponder the question for a moment and say, "I think I could go quite a while without a smoke!"

What made the difference? Their motivation was radically strengthened when they realized their life depended on their choice.

In our struggle against evil, we must

remember these are life-and-death issues! First, Jesus said to the disciples "Come unto me.." (Matthew 11:28) Then he told them that He possessed all power so that they could "Go" (Matthew 28:18, 19). We come to Jesus for mercy, grace and forgiveness then he gives us the power of the Holy spirit to go and live new lives and share everlasting life with others. We come to Him, and then Go for Him!

Learning to Walk

Few men have had a greater effect on modern times than Thomas Edison. In one lifetime he left our generation with a heritage of miraculous inventions that changed the world. From the light bulb to the phonograph, his little laboratory continued cranking out one marvel after another till it grew into the massive General Electric Corporation.

Edison was given credit for possessing rare and remarkable genius. In response he would say that most of his inventions were one per cent inspiration and 99 per cent perspiration. You see, in his attempt to perfect an invention, he failed many times, but he never gave up. Edison also said, "He that is afraid to fail is afraid to succeed." Whenever we attempt to reach a high goal, we risk a long fall.

In the same way, many people are afraid to take the steps of salvation because they might fail. So they never fulfill the great potential that God has for each one of us. Or they tried and failed once, so they're afraid to try again.

The Bible reminds us that even God's great heroes had their moments of failure and discouragement. But then they reached out and up to God for the resources and strength to pull themselves together and to press on and change the course of history.

I remember when my children were babies, I discovered there was a sequence in learning to walk. First they rolled over. Then they advanced to sitting and crawling. Eventually, they would stand and brace their shaky legs on pieces of furniture. Then they would let go and venture out into the great unknown, and usually they learned some bumpy lessons regarding the law of gravity. But that didn't keep them from trying time and time again!

When my children were learning to walk, and I saw them stumble and fall, do you suppose I picked them up, gave them a stinging smack, and said, "You clumsy child, you've fallen. Now don't you ever do that again?" Of course not! I was thrilled that they were attempting to walk toward me.

In teaching them to walk, I learned a secret. I would hand them a little toy or rattle, and I would hold one end while they held the other. We would then take a few steps together, but without their noticing, I'd let go and move out ahead. Pretty soon they would look at me across the room and then at the rattle swinging free in their hand. With a startled expression and a grin, they would continue to stumble forward to my open arms. Usually, after a couple of days of failing and getting up and trying again, they would take six or seven steps, and I could say they were walking! I would scoop them up in my arms and hug and praise them, and they'd squeal and giggle, and I'd toss them up in the air, and we would rejoice together.

In the same way, friends, your heavenly Father is waiting with outstretched arms. He'll help you take the steps where you tend to fall. He'll help you in your weak points. But don't be discouraged if you fall. Get back up, dust yourself off, and continue walking into the arms of your loving Saviour. As you draw near to God, He will draw near to you (James 4:8).

Dear friend, while you are reading these words, He is the one who is keeping your lungs breathing and your heart beating in your chest. He loves you so much that He died rather than to see you perish. He offers to take you back to a place where there is no sin, no sorrow, no suffering, no death or sadness–an everlasting life in bliss with pleasures forevermore (Revelation 21:4)!

Now if all this is true, nothing is more important than knowing Him and preparing yourself and others for His return! If it isn't true, then nothing really matters.

But I know it's true. Revelation 22:6 says, "These words are faithful and true."

The seven steps in this book found in Isaiah's conversion outline the science of salvation–a formula for faith. Let's review: (1) We must see God in the year our King Jesus died. After seeing God's goodness, our natural response is to, (2) see ourselves and our badness. The goodness of God then leads us to, (3) repent and (4) confess our sins. Immediately after that, we must (5) receive the cleansing and power our Lord freely offers. After our new birth, we have the desire and ability to (6) hear God's voice and finally (7) to follow wherever He may lead and go wherever He may send you.

These steps are much more than a process that we just experience one time at the beginning of our Christian walk. We need to see the Lord and examine ourselves on a daily basis. We must daily feel the need for repentance and confession as the Lord's prayer indicates. We can daily receive His forgiveness, daily listen for His voice, and daily make ourselves completely available to God by praying that prayer with Jesus, "Not my will, but they will be done" (Matthew 26:42).

"Ask, and it will be given to you; seek, and you will find; knock, and it will be opened to you. For everyone who asks receives, and he who seeks finds, and to him who knocks it will be opened" (Matthew 7:7,8).

Friend, don't you want to take these steps now and always? Eternal life and peace are only a prayer away! Why not pray now and receive the new life that Jesus offers?

GIVE ME A *HEART*

Lord, let me see with Your eyes
  Myself and all whom I meet.
I can go with Your sight through the darkest night,
  Lord, let me see with Your eyes.

Lord, let me speak with Your lips
  With kindness in all that I say,
Till everyone has heard of the hope in Your Word,
  Lord, let me speak with Your lips.

And, Lord, let me love with Your heart
  Come water the seed You have sown.
A miracle You must impart, dear Lord,
  Please give me a heart like Your own.

Lord, let me walk with Your feet
  Though narrow and strait be the way.
When the road goes uphill I will follow You still,
  Lord, let me walk with Your feet.

Lord, let me give with Your hands
  Remembering how much You gave.
Help me to give that others may live,
  Lord, let me give with Your hands.

And, Lord, let me love with Your heart
  All I have now is this heart of stone.
A miracle You must impart, dear Lord,
  Please give me a heart like Your own!

Doug Batchelor